Winning
Principles For Successful
Living

Motivational Nuggets for Winning

Precious-Ruth Barnes

Publisher House Ltd

© May 19th 2020 by Precious-Ruth Barnes.

First published by Publisher House Ltd. United Kingdom.

Tel: 07440061820

Email: publisherhouseltd@outlook.com

www.publisherhouseltd.com

All quotations are original content by author.

Typeset by Publisher House Ltd.

ISBN: 978-1-8380470-0-9

Introduction

I was going to start off by writing that we all need encouragement 'at times', however, I couldn't quite do that because I feel that's possibly not entirely true.

It's true, we need encouragement however, it's my belief that not a single person will ever have e-v-e-r-y-t-h-i-n-g perfectly in place at all times; and to that end, I resolve that we all need encouragement, all of the time.

There'll always be something that isn't completely quite how we'd like it to be. Whether as pertaining to our family life, relationships, finances, work and career; health, amongst many others, it may be safe to say that a sense of 'incompleteness' appears to be part of the packaging of life, and this is precisely the reason for this book.

Winning - Principles - for - Successful – Living.

Whether we are up or down, whether we feel accomplished or not; we must each get on with life regardless and therefore, the theme of this book is to encourage and reinforce in us that we can all win as we tackle life from the right perspectives.

Introduction

There are principles to act as guidelines to how we should think which can, if you like, be a 'buffer' that shields should life dish out what is far from our expectation. There are also principles that will encourage us to be bold go getters. The end point of it all being that we must have the right mindset in order to win in life.

There must be capacity in every person that enables them to continue standing when life brings storms; or capacity that enables a coming back when life knocks them down. In this book, we are reminded that this capacity is all in the mind. It's all about perspectives.

Winning Principles for Successful Living is packed with inspirational and motivational nuggets that will speak to the reader in many different ways. It's a book that almost gives you wings to fly. It is thought provoking with powerful nuggets that will have you thinking outside the box.

Some of the nuggets will help you love and appreciate 'you' more. Others, geared to shake us out of having a settler's mindset, challenge how we think passively when

Introduction

we've settled within our comfort zones; and gives wisdom principles to bring us out of settling.

Get reading! Feast your eyes and your mind on words of wisdom that will get you thinking positively differently with each quote. This book will kick start you to put a new value on yourself as you think differently by way of perspectives.

It is my hope that you will find this book to be a great read; as well as a handy tool that will impact you to have a better perspective about life, the value of life, situations of life and how you handle them.

Precious-Ruth Barnes

The Ten Commandments of Winning Principles:

- Live by Values and Principles.
- You live and you learn.
- Love loves and serves.
- Love is plain and simple. Love need not be complicated.
- Love is enough to keep our world in check; however there's not enough of it going around.
- If selflessness was a currency, the world would be a better place.
- The dictionary has never gone out of fashion! Use it.
- The world is not an island. Connect. Network.
- Don't ignore your conscience.
- As light is necessary to see, so is information. Stay current.

Tomorrow has a way of suddenly
turning up. Just as quickly, it dashes
past those who were
unprepared. Don't put anything
off till tomorrow. Do that thing
today. Do it now!

***

If everyone could have faith
in their neighbour, there'd
be such a strong bond formed. The
world wouldn't go wrong.

Advancement
comes with change.
Change is movement.

To accommodate change,
it may be necessary to
reinvent oneself
from
time to time.

Maintain the
right focus at all times.
Avoid distractions at all
cost. Always
keep your eyes, your
mind and your heart
steadfastly on your dream(s).

***

Be willing
to stretch. It is
generally the main way to get more
out of anything in life. It's called tenacity.

It doesn't matter
whether you
crawl, walk or run,
as long as you're not
standing still.

Keep pressing in
towards your dreams.

By the way,
do you have any dreams?
If not, then why not?

Visions become
clearer as you continue
to dream. Never stop
dreaming. Visualize what could be!

Ideas begin in the mind.
The place where seeming impossibilities
are given life.

***

It really doesn't matter what
motivates you to adopt,
adapt and stick to a good course.

Hashtag: Means to an end!

Effort put into anything
on an inconsistent
basis really isn't good
enough.

Inconsistency creates
gaps in a process
and may ultimately
require having to
start over.

Better be consistent
if you mean
to really give something
a shot.

Life. Win!
It is literally as simple
as that. You are either a winner in
life or you are not. Decide which
end of the spectrum
of life you'd like to be on. Success or
failure! Then just work for it.

***

No matter how you may
be feeling, wisdom
always thinks first before it acts.

Hashtag: Wise Actions! Wisdom! Be Wise!

Never cut corners
in your endeavours. It
will definitely come
back to bite you. If something
is going to take long to
accomplish, see that
as a sacrifice worth
making.

Never cut corners.

Do things the right way.
Always!

Having a positive mindset
will see you thrive where others
are dying.

***

For the optimist, there
is light everywhere; not just at the
end of the tunnel.

The challenge is to
find the light! Switch it on and use it
to find your way out quickly.

Hashtag: Determined to Win!

Conditions won't
always be perfect.

There will be rainy days.

Nevertheless,
sometimes, things have
just
got to get done.

Hashtag: Nevertheless attitude!

Mastery. Promotion. Elevation

You must have mastered and
surpassed your present level of
talent and skill before you can expect to
be moved up higher.

Hashtag: Competence!

***

Every day is the day you
could be made.
To avoid missing out, always be prepared.

Keep preparing yourself.
Keep sharpening your skillset.
The day will come when
opportunity will require
you to shine.

You must not be
caught off guard. You
certainly
don't want to give less than your
best at that time.

Hashtag:
When Opportunity Knocks!
Opportunities!

Always be present wherever
you are. Be present
in whatever you're doing or
else, don't be there at all.

Hashtag: Presence of mind!

***

There's experience
in every moment. Experiences
have benefit. Whether good
or bad, experiences are
tremendous teachers.

Don't get stuck in
life!

Learn new ways
to navigate through life in order
to make new
things happen for you.

Winning!

Re-load to re-fire

Reflection and rebranding
may be necessary at times.

Don't get stuck in life.

***

Be flexible enough
to stay relevant. Change is the currency
of being current.

Know that you NEED
information. Indeed knowledge is
power. With knowledge, you
stand at the door to
growth and change. Know more and
you can do more.

Identify how you learn best. Then
get cracking on. Get more information!

Knowledge is key to advancement in
anything. Get knowledge by getting
information. Add understanding in the
mix. Then, you stand a chance
at success in life.

What use
is it wallowing
in your
pains, disappointments
and regrets?

None whatsoever!

***

A winner's mindset
is one that turns minuses
to pluses.

24

Obsession
with scrutiny
can only produce
flawlessness and
excellence.

The trick is to maintain
whatever standard is
required to get a
job well done.

Remain steadfast with brilliance and
excellent
right till the end.

Don't let up!

Multiple streams of income is the new
normal. If you don't currently have one,
then consider how
to make this a reality in your life.
Then go after it
as if your life depends on it; because
in a way, your
life does depend on it.

***

You're doing yourself
an injustice, if you only
have one stream of income.
Add more to your
wealth in terms of income.

Define yourself! Know
who you are. What makes you tick?
What gives you joy?

Where and how do you
find your peace? What motivates you?
What keeps you sane?
What challenges you to be more, to do
more and grow?

Questions! Questions and
there are even more
more questions.

Bottom line is, know yourself; and stay
true to yourself.

Be a good manager
of whatever you have;
however small it
may be.

***

Promotion and
elevation comes from
how well you manage what
you currently have.

Be youself!

The world has no choice
but to adjust!

There is much truth in the saying
'experience is the best
teacher'

Be a student of life. Be resourceful. Good
or bad, allow yourself to be taught by life.

***

Do good.
To one person, in one situation at a time.
Then just repeat.

You want to be
sure you are being dealt
the best hand in life as much
as is possible.

Accepting anything less
is a
compromise.

Do not settle for a compromised life
or existence.

Uncap yourself. Take the
limits off. Put every good ability and skill
you possess to good use.
Ask yourself, why will you not fire on all
cylinders when you know you can?

***

Let change in whatever form you
encounter it, always change you for
the better. Never permit yourself to
go backwards in life.

Life comprises of many
different
personalities and
characters.

Don't be left out!

Let the world see you
in your true form.
Show up!

Let your life speak!

Want more out of life!
Dare ask for more. Worst case scenario; you
won't get what you asked for, but you
wouldn't have lost anything in asking.

Dare to dare! Life is for the taking. Hold
back and you may always be at the back,
making no progress.

***

Never hurry the process
of being or becoming excellent.
By the way, go again when you think you
have finished. You will find there will
always be more that you can give.

Consistency is actively applying
yourself to something even if it's only
a little bit at a time.
It is making sure
you don't miss a step.

Being consistent may not
always be easy however,
herein lies the very
essence of consistency. Keeping
things going regardless.

Resources!
Be a collector of information,
however don't just collect
information. Do put your
collection to use.

***

Be an optimist.
Use challenges of life as
stepping stone to shift gear and
move you to higher heights.

It costs nothing to be
an optimist. One that's
always hopeful;
always expecting the
Best.

It may cost everything
being a pessimist.

Making no room for
possibilities. Being a closed
door to what could be.

A pessimist's mind is constantly shrouded in negatives. When confronted with a challenge, the pessimist gives up in their mind right from the outset; often without being open to give thought to possibilities.

Having already given up in the mind, the pessimist lets themselves down every time as they close the door to explore possibilities to obtain solutions.

***

Be an optimist. Give yourself a chance.

Life becomes
restricted and grounded
where there are no
dreams or aspiration to
achieve great feats.

Get serious about life
will you?
Play time is so over.

***

They do say never take
yourself too seriously!

Learn to strike a balance.

Work, Rest and Play.

Very vital to successful
living.

An imbalanced lifestyle is
dangerous and will
ultimately affect your
productivity negatively.

Have a visual of the type of
life you would like. It
will help to keep
you in check and
motivated

***

Put in front of you
what you want.

Hashtag: Visual Motivation

Wealth and luxury
gives a fantastic
level of comfort in life.

You are deserving of
wealth!

Have a wealthy mindset!

You can choose to settle for a 9 to 5 job or its equivalent of something that pays by the hour or a salary that is always never enough!

Hashtag: Multiple Streams of Income!

***

You could decide that you would like to have a stake in the wealth of the world. Ask yourself... 'What will it take?'

Read this entire page again!

Plan for new initiatives.

You don't have
to keep doing the
same things for years.
Be in the same
profession for twenty years.

You are permitted to
change. Do something different.
Do you see the world
evolving around you?

Stretch your boundaries so you can
do more. Dream bigger dreams.
Aspire to achieve greater
feats. Envisage great things then go for it.
Truly the world is an oyster to those who
dare to dream.

***

Great enterprises we know of
In our time were initiated
by humans
just like you and I.

People with a cup 'half full'
mindset use what they have to
gain more whilst people with a
cup 'half empty'
mindset sit on what they have;
rather than using it to leverage.

This is perspectives. This is
mindsets.

It's optimism versus pessimism.
Which one would you really
rather be?

Ask all the right
questions that will assist
you to go forward in life.

***

Innovators make
our world go round. They
dream and birth
things that become necessities
for everyday living.

How will you be remembered? What
will you be remembered for? Or perhaps
you really don't care to be remembered.

48

Capacity is like elastic. It can be stretched.

Wherever you're at in life; you can always do more. You can always do better.
You are not limited to only what you can already do.
Do more.

Think elastic!

Stretch! Push!

Being consistent will
require that we be people of discipline.
Herein lies the true
essence of being consistent. Keeping
on whether one feels like it or not.

***

Consistency is what
gets you the result you want.
You must be consistent In order to
maintain being consistent.

Be a disruptor
of status quo, if it
means
you living at your
maximum potential.

You must, must, emerge!

Whatever Job you are currently qualified to do is good enough for today. As it is necessary in life, give that job your very best.

That said however, in life, you should always aim for more. Never just settle where you are. If you decide to do more, you can always do more.

***

Don't just exist in life.

It is never too late or too
early to make a change.

You can quit anything you shouldn't
be doing at any time.

You never have to continue on
endlessly on a wrong path. Make
that change.
Make that change *NOW!*

Have the courage to begin a new walk if
that's what's required.

A better you will benefit you and
all who come in contact with you.
Be a plus!

***

Rub shoulders with people who inspire
and encourage you to be a better version
of your current self.

The only restriction to your
self-improvement is often the man in the
mirror.
Uncap yourself. Uncap your potential.

Self-improvement
is limitless. You can always be better.

If you spend a long enough time on a puzzle, you will figure it out. However, it will require dedication and commitment. Such is the principle that must be applied to life.

***

Don't just go through the motions of life being a collector of number in years.
Read that again!

Life could be so much more, however you have to really want it.

Never concern yourself
with; never get
preoccupied with; and never give
yourself or your focus
to anything that can draw you away
from something that's good
and working for you.

In other words, manage
and protect you focus.

You are not necessarily matured
because you've accumulated
number in years. Neither are you
immature because you're young in age.
Sometimes common sense is
not so common and life happens to all.
The main thing is to make your life count.

***

Your time to shine is always
now. Think about it! You won't
get this moment back once it's gone. Time
to put your best foot forward is always now.

Ask positive
questions that will
give answers that are
solutions to you moving
forward
in life.

Avoid dwelling on
negative thoughts or
memories
that stroke your
hurts; and keep you
attached to regrets and pains.

***

Learn to preserve energy
by
maintaining your focus.

Speak positivity into your situation.
Speak power into your situation.
Speak life into your situation.

If you'll spend effort and energy,
let it be for good.

Be a builder with your words. Not
one that tears down.

Don't waste energy or effort
spewing out negativity.
Speak good into your situation.
Speak life.

Consistent gradual
building is great. It will
get the job done. It will also keep
you from burn-out.

***

Rome wasn't built in a day. Be satisfied
when you're doing the best you can

Go easy on yourself.

You have choices
in life. Be ordinary;
or aim to do
something
great and make an
impact with your life.

Eliminate comfort zones from
your mind; from your life.
Refuse to be ordinary.

After all, *WHY* be ordinary?

***

Information is everything.
Don't remain ignorant
and uninformed. Get
information in order to stay ahead.

Surround yourself with the right people.

People who support you and who encourage you to grow and be the best that you can be.

Let integrity be the reason
why you won't let people
down.

***

A present challenge
shouldn't change your mind or plan
about your ultimate life's goal.

Don't be a push over.

Roll up your sleeves, roll up your
cocks and get on with the task
at hand.

Take your time and
BE excellent.
Pace yourself and BE excellent.

Smile your way as you
pursue being excellent.

Excellence is a
great standard to strive for
and to have.

If you want your life to count, you
must go all out.

Hashtag: No Limitations!
Soar with Eagles!

***

Be nice. Be kind.

It may be all some people need. In
which case, it will make a
huge impact. It will also cost you nothing.

No matter what unfortunate
circumstances you
have seen in life; you have power in
your hands.

Make up your mind that you
are not a victim of unfortunate
circumstances of life.

Decide that you are always a victor.

It pays to have the right mind
frame.

Doing so propels you to reach for; and
attain unto heights
that you will have otherwise not dared
to reach for.

***

Make no room for limitations.

Understand that
unless it's a deliberate desire
to fail at what
you do, everything
that you put your mind and
effort to is
achievable and attainable.

Step up and step out.
Put in the work.
Pay the sacrifice.

Pay attention to yourself.
See yourself as someone special and
show yourself
in your true form.

***

There isn't just one set way to do life
successfully. Explore
the different ways available to win
in order to keep winning daily.

Stretch! Enough to
get out of procrastination. Stretch!
Enough to get out of comfort zones.

Stretch!
Rise up above limitations.

Stretch, because your
growth can be limitless and boundless.

Evaluate the people that you have
in your life.

It should be that you
have more of the kind of people
who add value to your life
and you to theirs.

***

Our associations should always
enrich us in one way or another.

People who challenge
us directly and indirectly participate
in our growth process.

You and I should also be
such persons in the lives
of other people.

We should individually be
valuable assets to life and society.

Profit and progress
in life comes when we maintain
consistency in doing more of the right
things and less of the wrong ones.

***

Words are very powerful.

Consider that it's far
better to say nothing if your words
will have a hurtful and damaging
impact in any way.
Do good!

Even if all participants in a race
were of excellent calibre, there is
nevertheless only one
gold medal.

There will always
be distinction. For certainly, there
are always differences and
levels of excellence.

Complacency is a killer. It will keep you small when you should be a giant. Don't settle!

***

When you know you can do more, in terms of your capability, capacity and, potential steer clear of everything and everyone that cannot fathom that possibility.

Do not allow associations to hinder possibilities in your life.

Tough times
won't kill you.
They will just
make you stronger
and better!

If you happen upon a
mountain in your life's journey, the
challenge will be to work out
how to get to the other side.
The answer is *NOT TO QUIT*.

***

You'll inevitably be strengthened
and become wiser by the difficult
challenges and circumstances
that you go through.

How ironic is that? Difficult times
won't kill you. They'll just make
you better.

There is always
untapped potential
lying dormant within you.

You can add more value
to yourself at any time. Study
something new. Upgrade or refresh
on your current
skillset.

***

We should be looking
to do all of our
talking with our actions.

Do
whatever you
must to
protect and maintain
your peace.

Your gifts and abilities
is your potential that can
be put to profitable use.

To that end, have you paid any
attention to your gifts and abilities lately?

***

Don't cheat yourself
being anything other than who you
are meant to be. Stay
in your lane. Apply yourself. Be
diligent and succeed.

Successful people
have a language. It is
that of self-belief,
self-confidence. Perseverance,
dedication and determination.
A no quitting
no matter what attitude.

Choose which language
you speak because it
will produce the
corresponding fruit
in your life.

Raise your standard.
Make yourself 'more' valuable.

***

Consider anything and anyone
that strokes and pampers
you in your weakness an adversary.

You'll never know how
strong you can be, if you don't go
through 'your' particular
seasons of difficult process.

You'll have to pull
your best punches if you want
to win any fight.

To that end, one way or another,
battles bring out the
best in you.

You're not going to
make a mark in life if you are the
same as everyone else. Know
your difference. Be different and
make your mark.

***

False humility is a lie
and confusion. Never underrate
having self-belief and
self-confidence. Recognize and put
value on your strengths.

Excellence is the
highest form of order.

Excellence!

It doesn't come easy. It cannot
be attained haphazardly;
and it won't come without
being meticulous.

Excellence must be maintained
in order to maintain the high
standard of excellence.

There are levels of excellence
because excellence is measurable.

There are levels of quality,
because quality is also measurable.

***

Good timing is being
in the right place at the
right time; but can you discern that
good timing must be perceived?

Come differently if you want
to stand out.

Standing out is
being outstanding.

Come correct if you want to be
noticed. Correctness demands
you to be thorough.

***

Correctness is preparedness.
Preparedness is correctness.

Promotion and advancement requires
correctness.
Promotion and advancement
demands preparedness.

Hashtag: Come correct!

Life has a system
and principle of
sowing and reaping.

A time waster should
expect unproductivity
as the fruit and result
of time wasted.

If you respect time and use wisely
you can then expect to
see productivity and good results
in your life.

Hashtag: Respect Time!

***

Some ventures are risks worth
taking. Think, 'no pain, no gain'.

Truthfully, sometimes, the best things are
those you'll have to fight for.

The successes or
failures of our lives will
be in consonance
with principles
we've applied and values we have
observed.

The best part of life's
struggles and difficult circumstances,
is going through and coming out
triumphant.

Life won't always be a bed of
roses, however, you can choose to be
an overcomer *ALL* of the time.

***

Take what you have now
and work with it from where you now.
Believe this; everyone always has
something that they can work with now!

One day at a time.
One step at a time.
One effort at a time.

Little by little, if you believe
that you can; you will get
things together.

Keep building. Keep things going!

Never give up!
Just think, one step at a time.

You will not
successfully manage being great
unless you have order
and being organized in place.

Be organized and
let there be order.

***

There is coming a time
when it will be your turn to shine and
you will have to be ready.
Never stop preparing or improving on
yourself.

Outside the remits of the
law, compassion and care,
never permit anyone
to cap your potential by
telling you what
you can and cannot do.

Ask yourself, why not you?

Why must it be someone else?
What will you be
known for?

Put out your own blueprint in your time.

The choice is yours
as to whether you are worthy of
sophistication and class.

Place value
on yourself.

***

Be marketable. Be remarkable.
Be valuable. Be profitable.

Be organized! It helps to
improve productivity.
It brings structure.

Structure aids focus.

Focus is key to implementation; and
eliminates time wasting.

Let's get organized.

Nothing changes unless you change it.
Nothing happens until
you do something. Talk not backed by
action is mere talk. Let's walk our talk.

***

To be effective and make maximum impact,
we must do the *right thing* at the *right time*.

Endeavour to understand the 'what' aspect
of different seasons; and the 'why' aspect
of timing.
To everything, there is a
season and a time for every endeavour.

Your decision making
process is likely to
be impaired if you
aren't thinking
right.

Declutter your mind!

Sometimes, just put pressure on
yourself to do more than your usual.
Hashtag: Discipline!

***

Sometimes discipline is just being hard
on yourself. Waking up
earlier. Perhaps, sticking
at something a little longer. Putting off
the good life till later. In the
end the cost of discipline is always
worth paying.

Hashtag: Pay the price!

Allocate time
appropriately to ensure you have
a well-balanced life.

Work hard. Play hard.
Be effective and productive. Strike the
right balance and remember;
all work and no play, makes for a
dull life.

A balanced and well-rounded life,
makes a successful and fulfilled life.

Abundance and surplus is great.
Having more than enough is fantastic.

Aim for the best of what's
available. Aim big, not small.

Have more than you need so
you can touch the lives of others.
Insufficiency benefits no one.

Hashtag: Wealth!

***

THINK OUTSIDE THE BOX

Greatness is birthed
from being
uncomfortable
with your present circumstances.

Be the change you want to see.

If you're convincing enough, you might impact someone else to also make a change.

***

Choose a life of no limitation.
Learn to soar like the eagles. Always push yourself out a little more than you've done before.

Hashtag: The go getter!

At what point?
is it impossible to become great?

If you'll just keep climbing, you'll
find you're getting higher.

Aspire for greatness
See big. Dream big.

Aim very high and
you won't fall short

Winning is all about playing
fabulously well whatever hand
you're dealt.

***

Never dim your light for anyone
who cannot handle your spark.

The sun goes down when
it's time to go down, not when people
complain it's too hot.

Do what you've got to
Do; and keep doing it well.

There must be
distinction. Always!

There must be a
difference. Always!

There must be
diversity in the arena of
being the best.

Trust is such a
valuable commodity.
It is one of the main things to
determine
whether we get moved
up to the next level
in our field of endeavour;
be that work or pleasure.

***

Diversity of opinions is
so rich and vital to
growth. Analyse them and you'll see
vast potential for innovation.

Your victory begins
from the moment
you recognize
and acknowledge that
there is a problem.

In a garden of roses and
beautiful flowers, identify the weed
so you know what must be uprooted
and killed.

Hashtag: Know the real deal.

***

Pruning is necessary
to make room
for emergence of
the new,
in even better form.

In a world of cause
and effect, don't
be afraid to sow. You will
reap!!!

Do ensure you
sow the right seed.

Do good. Do right.
Have good manners,
character and attitude.
Be kind.
Be generous.
Love people and
show compassion.

You cannot claim expertize in your field
of endeavour and be fearful of change or
the unknown.

An expert must be able
to consistently produce
(from scratch);
and reproduce.

Hashtag: Know your craft!
Hone your craft!

***

Be confident in who you are. Have
faith in what you can do.

To get ready is to sharpen
your tools. To stay ready
is to
remain relevant.

Hashtag: Be relevant!
Remain relevant!

When presented with a
challenge to do something you
don't know how to do;
think, I can learn. Think, I will
learn. Think possibilities!

Think anything other than I can't'.

***

As pertaining to the
accomplishment of any
endeavour, if the mind isn't first
prepared, the will won't co-operate
to get the job done.

If given a thought, the
bottom line of saying 'I can't'
is 'I don't want to try'.

Remove constraints
on yourself.

Nothing is impossible
when you put your mind to it.

Totally eliminate 'I can't'
from your vocabulary; Exchange
'I can't' with I will learn how.

Your mind carries much
power to direct how your ship sails.
It's always a case of the mind over matter.

Whatever the mind decides is
what will be achieved. Arm yourself fully
with the power of your mind. Think right
and win!

***

You win or lose first in
your mind.

Read that again!!!

Printed in Great Britain
by Amazon

55734925R00068